A Moment in Time

Wendy

BookLeaf
Publishing

Presentation by *BookLeaf Publishing*

Web: www.bookleafpub.com

E-mail: info@bookleafpub.com

ISBN: 9789357615822

First edition 2022

DEDICATION

For Leisl

Just a Cat

"She's just a cat."
Stoicism, in the face of reality.

"She's just a cat."
Naïveté, from a life led too easy.

"She's just a cat."
Tenacity, for the fear of exposure.

"She's just a cat."
Disbelief, as I cradled serenity.

"She's just a cat."
Deception, for the truly heartbroken.

The Girl

What became of the girl who used to climb trees
 who used to run wild and swore never to leave
 The rusting playground, once more on the
swings

 What became of the girl who used to draw
creatures
 from mythical lands, with impossible features
 Deadly eyes, three horns, a kaleidoscope of
colour

 What became of the girl who used to make
nests
 of weeds and thick mud, for evening birds to lay
rest
 Never did she think that her presence deterred
them

 The girl, she grew up, as all girls must do
 in this Peter Pan, Wendy-bird matured, too
 But it was a choice, don't say it's inevitable
 The marks from a childhood are truly indelible

adult

What is an adult?
someone who rejoices in
fuel efficiency

Phantom

There once was a kitten lost and found in the bushes,
 Who loves to run wild and our patience he pushes
 A jiu jitsu practice
 Each claw like a cactus
 With meows silenced frequently by many shushes

deconstruction

it is not hate i feel but loss
 for what friendship with you cost
 why anger and daggers
 you choose to blind stagger
 the peace that you want
 not in poisonous taunts

it is not hate i feel but loss.
goodbye.

Red-Rumped Parrot

What a name for a bird
A fleeting delight
Of teal and bright yellows
And a namesake red back

What a name for a bird
Such a sight to behold
Flitting and swooping
Creativity unmatched

Our Words, Deficient

Many pens and many pages
Ink spilt across the ages
Confess what is known to stand
The greatness of the perfect Man

And though undeserving
His mercy unswerving
Condescended for the rebellious
The obstinate, the self-righteous

Now redeeming the things declared broken
Reconciled in grace, these words He has spoken
To know such love, joy, and peace sufficient
Our articulation with words, deficient

solace

to have a good friend
 and delight in their embrace
 "the finest balm" known.

driving playlist

you made it on
  with a thrumming beat and eerie refrains
  to the driving playlist
  that washes with nostalgic energy
  as the road stretches thin
  before me in ecstasy

  because on you the moon is but a pearl
  stolen from your mother's bedside

separate body

what is this i cannot shake
 i felt myself in time and space
 an entirely separate body
 stuck in the hotel lobby
 on a holiday gleaned off distant dreams
 with joy bursting from my seams

void

avoiding the issue
 voided procedures
 voided means of access
 voided contracts
 voided people
 i scream into the void

generosity

what is kindness and its sisters
of grace and generosity
to give as the sun does to the earth
nurturing growth with effortless warmth
to love as a mother does with her child
anxious from a joyful heart that overflows

dymocks

endless possibilities in the nook of a basement
tempting allures and sleek satin covers
a refuge amongst the tempest of work
wholly immersed in treasuring a purchase

so sudden

how could i know that you were moments away
that your visit to us was such a short stay
you were trying to tell us but we didn't know
in you was cancer the poisonous growth

i thought i had you for many years yet
many more memories now i simply forget
desperately sifting and clinging to you
leisl in death i know heartbreak proves true

today

today was a good day because the sun shone
  because my legs walked
  because my lungs breathed
  because my heart beat
  because i laughed from a place deep within
  because i sung while i walked home from the
bus
  because the neighbour's cat let me pat him
  because i drank green rose tea
  because my taxes are finally done
  because Flightless Bird is a great song
  because my husband plays music so beautifully
  because i am reconciled to my Creator.

lactose intolerant

it was really only a matter of time
 before i knew milk would be my great crime
 defiant, i wish i hated this new life more
 but it's great having a stomach not sore
 probiotics didn't help with my constant bloat
 for those with the enzyme, go on you can gloat

5 years

how can i love you
 so much more across the years
 than at the altar?

I Sat on the Edge

I sat on the edge, the precipice of light and dark.
 Between frostbitten sunlight and a teasing cold.
 Between obligations, duties and unwarranted
rest.

 I sat on the edge, between summer and autumn.
 Between stocking feet, cotton dresses and
woollen jumpers.
 Between warm, homemade lunches and cherry
potted yoghurts.

 I sat on the edge, a heart cradled in simplistic
notes.
 Between narratives and stories written to break.
 Between melodies that stung and lyrics that
wrecked.

 I sat on the edge, decision in my teeth.
 Between the whispers of nostalgia and the surge
of excitement.
 Between fresh beginnings and imminent
goodbyes.

 I sat on the edge, thinking of you.

Between the feelings packed away and the years
marked done.
 Between the okays and future optimisms that
just weren't quite that.

 I sat on the edge.